BLUES FOR A MUSTANG

Grant Guy

Blues for a Mustang
Copyright © 2018 Grant Guy

All rights reserved. Red Dahlia Press
is a subsidiary of Red Dashboard LLC Publishing
retains right to reprint this book. Permission to reprint
these poems elsewhere must be obtained from the author.

ISBN-13: 978-1-970003-28-4

Cover photography © 2018 was a musing from
*Saving America's Mustangs. The Foundation
For the Preservation of America's Wild Horses*
by Grant Guy with Michael Baca, Art Director
Cover design © The Red Dahlia Press
Biography Photo © Leif Norman

Published by Red Dahlia Press
Princeton NJ 08540
www.thereddahliapress.com

Home of the Red Dahlia Chapbook Prize

Some of the poems included in *BLUES FOR A MUSTANG* have appeared in the following publications;

ON WATCHING CHASING TRANE (Tuck Magazine), He Can Walk (Hidden Constellations) PICTURE OF JESUS and GOING OUT FOR ICE CREAM (Babbling The Irrational), THE RAINS CAME DOWN, HE WAS A GUNSLINGER, LONESOME COWBOY, HYMN FOR PAT GARRETT, JOHN SYMONS, POEM FOR FRANKLYN, ALL SHE ATE, HELL and HE HAD DREAMS (In Between Hangovers), BARB and DEATH CHANGED THE WAY HE LOOKED UPON THE WORLD (Harbinger Asylum), MINGUS and JAZZ NOTES (Duane Poetree), HE DANCED AT THE DROP OF A NOTE (Peeking Cat), IN A SMALL HOTEL ROOM (Poetic Diversity), ROAD KILL (Creative Talent Unleashed), POEM NO.2, MONK and COPYRIGHT INFRINGEMENT (Prairie Journal), MY DEALER OF ILLUSIONS, WINTER, SOUNDING POST, THE PEARLY GATES and I REACH OUT (Outlaw Poetry), PRETTY BOY FLOYD KNEW, HOBO and He Loved (Scarlet Leaf Review), FATHERS (Poetry Poetic Pleasures), MARKET & MAIN, he can walk and SHE JUST DID and LOVE RUNS LIKE DRY SEX, THERE IS A HELL (Spillwords), THE TALL PRAIRIE GRASS WAS IN HIS LANGUAGE (Winnipeg Free Press), BUS 5612(Bus Stop Bus Stop, Red Dashboard), THE SAD CUP OF COFFEE (On The Bright Side of Down, Red Dashboard), POEM #8, I DRINK HARD ENOUGH WHEN I AM SOBER and NOTHING TO SAY TO THE WORLD (Literary Yard), HANGING SAM (Poetry Super

Highway), he said do you need a dollar (The Open Mouse), ON A TRIP TO DISNEY WORLD (Dissident Voice), NOTHING NEW UNDER THE SUN, NO REGRETS and THE VIETNAMESE RESTAURANT (The Wagon Magazine), 1875 and MONGREL WORDS (Stanzaic Stylings), NOTHING NEW UNDER THE SUN, NO REGRETS and VIETNAMESE RESTAURANT (The Wagon Magazine), WHEN MY FATHER MOUNTED MY MOTHER and FAMILY ALBUM (Your One Phone Call), SHE SAID I SAID, IN A WORLD WHOSE HEART HAS BEEN EXTRACTED, HIS STORY: AN OBSERVATION and SHE SLEEPS SOUNDLY BESIDE ME (Beatnik Cowboy)

TABLE OF CONTENTS

On Watching Trane 3
Nothing New Under the Sun 4
No Regrets 4
The Vietnamese Restaurant 5
in a world whose heart
      has been extracted 6
He Was a Gunslinger 7
The Lonesome Cowboy 8
His Story: An Observation 9
Mongrel Words 10
Nothing New Under the Sun 11
Love Runs Like Dry Sex 12
Barb 13
death changed the way
      he looked at the world 14
My Dealer of Illusions 15
Winter 16
Sounding Post 17
She Sleeps Soundly Beside Me 18
She Said, I Said 19
Poem No 2 20
Jazz Notes 21
letting my guard down 22
it had gotten to the point 23
the cowboy died
      a long time before he died 24
Market and Main 25
There Is A Hell 27

The Pearly Gates 28
I Reach Out 29
Sad Cup of Coffee 30
he said do you need a dollar 31
Copyright Infringement 32
Monk 33
Hanging Sam 34
While Horseback Riding 35
Road Kill 36
Bus 5612 37
On a Trip to Disney World 38
Pretty Boy Floyd Knew 39
Family Album 40
The Rain Came Down 41
Poem for Franklyn 42
All She Ate 44
Hell 45
She Just Did 46
It Is Best 47
A Wider World 48
Hymn for Pat Garrett 49
1959 50
Times Are Always the Same
    'Cept When Times A'changin' 51
Baked Beans With Crow 52
1875 53
Bunchgrass 54
John Symons 55
Poem No 4 56
Poem No 5 57
Cowboy Art 58

A Buffalo Rode
    Across His Soul Each Night ………………….. 59
He Was Thirsty the Day He Died ………………… 60
Butch Cassidy ………………… 61
He Had Dreams ……………….. 62
He Danced at the Drop of a Hat ……………….. 63
In a Small Hotel Room ……………….. 64
The Beatnik Cowboy ………………. 65
Hobo ………………. 66
The Tall Prairie Grass
    Was in His Language ………………. 67
he can walk ………………. 68
Fathers ………………. 69
When My Father Mounted My Mother ……………….. 70
Pictures of Jesus ………………. 71
Going Out for Ice Cream ………………. 72
Mingus ………………. 73
Poem No 8 ………………. 74
I Drink Hard Enough
    When I Am Sober ………………. 75
Nothing to Say to the World ………………. 76

On Watching Trane

The first time
The first time
The very first time
    & God knows not the last time
I had a hard time to forgive my race
The Birmingham Church bombing
That took the life 4 young girls

I don't think I have forgiven my race.

And the bodies keep piling up
In the name of a white man
In the name of a white God
In the name of a white dollar

No Regrets

Let's do something tonight
Unlike my momma and the preacher man
Will have nothing to regret

When I become totally impotent
Like a car up on blocks
And you like a dried prune
In the dog days of summer
Our love will still be fueled with passion

Let's do something tonight

The Vietnamese Restaurant

The owner
Of the Pho Quyhn
She stood at the end of the table
Shaking her finger at a customer
Have not seen you for long time
You must be seeing someone else

in a world whose heart has been extracted

in a world whose heart has been extracted from hope
i am on my own w/o a name or face
i stand in my naked clothes of deception
behind a dead mic

i howl & howl & whimper & whimper
to an empty space w/o dimensions
but no one no one has come to hear me

my words are the empty words of a dying antonin artaud
sputtering meaningless syllable & yaps for hours on end

cruelty and kindness are dismembered
& thrown like johnny's appleseeds
into the long loneliness of the void beyond nothing

b/c i am god's orphan

He Was A Gunslinger

He was a gunslinger with no last name
Most of the men who died at the end of his barrel
Did not even know his last name
The reasons is because   No men died at the end of his barrel

The thing that burnt him most

Hollywood never came calling
   Every day he checked his emails
In the lobby of Motel 6

The woes of being a modern-day cowboy

The Lonesome Cowboy

The lonesome cowboy
Was lonesome because he did not drink.
Even his horse laughed at him,
"What kind of cowboy are you?
Can't get drunk enough to fall off your horse."

It was then the lonesome cowboy
Gave up the ranching life.
Moved to the big city.
Became an accountant for a large firm.

Died an alcoholic in 1907.

Last words: Trigger. Trigger.

His Story: An Observation

His wife's stroke he turned it into a story being all about him
His father-in-law's funeral became all about him.
When Reagan was shot it was definitely a story about him
Oh, let us not forget about his sister dying from leukemia
Nor to mention the molestation and murder
of the 69-year-old housewife
The Blue Jays winning the World Series
The bus plunge in El Salvador

in his mind they were all about him
That was the kind of guy he was

So when he died
And no one showed up

It was all about him

Mongrel Words

Mongrel words ingest the harmony of poetry
Bequeathing it with a reality of sinew and bone

The misfit words are the rising citadel
That bares the cradle of short range dreams of men & women
Bulldozing the long-range plans

Every day I chew on the malcontented words
Nourishing me with the spine and raw muscle
  to kiss the morning
To hug the night in gracious avidity

I drink the miscued words with unquenching thirst
I stride up to the bar of life and grab another bottle
I cannot get enough of the bullets and knives they heaves
At the reality of our blue ball lost in space
For the molesting words are psalms

Without the menacing words the harmony of poetry is spat out

We are as dead as the void without a godhead

Let us be possessed by misbecoming words

Nothing New Under the Sun

They jaywalked from Eaton's to The Met.
He was thirsty.
She was cold.
Waving his arms,
And saying as loud as he could,
"You don't understand.
There's nothing new under the sun.
We can only do it better."

He was still waving his arms
When he stepped into a pothole
And somersaulted on the road,
His heels hit the curb.

She said,
"I've seen that before,
But can you do it better next time."

Love Runs Like Dry Sex

Love runs like dry sex
She walked in & out of love
Opening & shutting the door before & after her

In the beginning
I thought a miracle was about to happen
There was a miracle for the secular kind
Not the miracle I had expected

The miracle
The miracle was how little I was hurt
After falling 18 stories of love

Barb

it is 3:30 am
except for the truck stop along the transcanada
in northern ontario
all   everyone is asleep   dead

the short order cook coughs over the grill
something flew out of his mouth

barb & tina are not talking about their dead children
barb & tina are talking about the church picnic next sunday

tina confesses she has a crush on the pastor

barb   well   she ...

barb moves to the front of the counter
to pick up a napkin discarded on the floor
as she is about to pick up the napkin
she sees jack pulling his rig into the yard

barb thinks of her dull husband
her face blank as the void
she thinks of Jack
her eyes light up like the morning sky

barb steps to the truckers' showers at the back
she enters shower #3
& she needs Jack
& god will still love her

death changed the way
        he looked upon the world

death changed the way he looked upon the world
                        sure   yes yes
he knew he would never see another july sunrise
nor take in the scent of newly mown grass
or be stung by a bumble bee

he knew all this & more

he had envisioned what death would see

he never thought
death be another kind of world

not to see a damn thing
that was the piss off

well next time he will be better prepared
                              he thought

what

there is no next time

My Dealer of Illusions

My dealer of illusions slipped out the backdoor
While I was putting the coffee on

I am the old woman who lived in a shoe of verse
I was the drunken hunchback in the park
With a bottle at my lips looking for words
The bottle was drier than an August desert
Like a California poet I bedded
Five hundred metaphors in one year

I applied all the poets' tricks of the trade
  I learnt in sidewalk cafes
Or on the top floor in an attic of poetic rubbings
All the skills of my craft were useless as truth in a cop shop

Still I dab at the blank paper b/c the scribbling
Of bandaged sentences may find a path
Into the warm yellow sun . . .

Winter

Winter in the country is white as Heaven
Winter in the city is dirty like Life

I know where I want to go when I am dead

Sounding Post

Leroy Jenkins
Leroy Jenkins
Leroy Jenkins
Draw that bow across the strings of virtue

Leroy Jenkins
Leroy Jenkins
Leroy Jenkins
Wail that song shouting out onto a grey world

Leroy Jenkins
Leroy Jenkins
Leroy Jenkins
Bring home the chords of the human mystery

Of life
Of the Universe

Shake hands with eternal soul

She Sleeps Soundly Beside Me

I reached out to her but she was gone
She sleeps soundly beside me
Our voice had stopped kissing in the fog of time
She sleeps soundly beside me

I kept my hands in my pocket
When she needs a hand to reach the zenith
She sleeps soundly beside me
The hot afternoon of love flows
As a river to the vast ocean
She sleeps soundly beside me

Now bitter tongues remain silent in the halls of romance
She sleeps soundly beside me
Our words are bullets of dystopic of open wounds
She sleeps soundly beside me

She sleeps soundly beside me

And I nightmare in exchange

She Said. I Said

She said, "Ever used cocaine?"
I said, "No."
She said, "It will make you really horny."
I thought to myself,
She wants me."
She snorted to show me how it is properly done.
I snorted.
   I fell asleep.

She went to the bar and got laid.

Poem No 2

It was hard to ignore him
like the efficiency of a swiss coo coo clock

He said
    Freud was wrong
    Einstein was wrong
    Foucault was wrong
    Chomsky was wrong
    etc.
    etc.
    etc.

They were all
Ronald McDonald thinkers

In North America
we are what we eat
in Europe they are what they read

Jazz Notes

Monk said,
"You know what's the loudest noise in the world, man?
The loudest noise is silence."

To quote someone, I don't remember who,
"How true, how true, how true."

letting my guard down

open your heart to love she sd
let your guard down she sd
But i have her ways of passion before
it cuts like obsidian to the gristle of one's being

i move away from her   keeping my eyes on her
i will not let my guard down on her terms of love
i did not see her love's sister   hate in the shadows
plunges a stiletto into my guarded body

maybe letting my guard down
maybe letting my guard down

it's too late to know now

it had gotten to the point

it had gotten to the point
that i couldn't believe a word God sd

it has become so bad
i stopped believing in the old fellow

but
christ was i stupid
i totally forgot
god is an ambusher
he got me between the eyes
he got me along the interstate 44
between tulsa & oklahoma city

now
now
he expects me to go to sunday school

the cowboy died
      a long time before he died

the day he died was not the day the cowboy stopped dancing
the cowboy died a long time before he died
& he quit dancing long before he quit dancing
he stopped being a cowboy before he stopped dancing

to be a man he had to earn a nest egg—
that's what the magazines & tv shows told him
he began to judge men by the character of their wallet

none of this concerned his wife of 25 years
she hadn't seen or talked to him for a decade
she never knew why she loved him 25 years ago
she forgot if she ever had
the last time she talked to him he threw a phone book at her

she left to have a life

&

he sat on his nest egg
he sat on his wallet waiting for his investments to hatch

Market and Main

I was on my way home from work
Crossing Market and Main
A drunk made a bee-line straight for me
His hand was outstretched

He asked for spare change to buy a cup of coffee
We were standing outside a liquor store
I knew it was not coffee he wanted

Having just found a wallet
With sixty dollars inside
I bought the drunk a bottle of wine

Instead of a polite tipping of the hat
And a giving me God bless you
He accompanied me in my walk
Across Main Street
And on toward Portage

He mumbled about this and that
Until he finally said

Have you heard of Che Guevera
Being a Marxist

Of course I know whom Che Guevera was

> Well, I fought with Che in the Sierra Maestra of Cuba
> back in '59.

I said Uh huh

He added

Look at Fidel Castro now
He's the president of his country
And I'm only a fucking drunk

There Is A Hell

There is a hell
A hell worse than any dreamt by Dante
A hell of loneliness in a crowded room

The Pearly Gates

When you get to Heaven
don't expect to See No St. Peter

He ain't there
He went to the other place
Except there is no other place
Wherever the He is
JC ain't got a freakin' clue
His faith was too narrow
Exclusive like a Men's Club

No   When you get to the Pearly Gates   Ha
You will see Thomas or Judas smoking dope
They found what was within
Took it for a walk in the sun

Thomas and Judas would tell the dearly departed souls
Go away   Don't ever come back
You saw the Kingdom of Heaven within
You already got it
Ain't nothin' for you here
Move along

Then Thomas and Judas laughed at
The paradox of the whole damn lot

I Reach Out

I reach out across the seconds and hours to find you
But you are alert as a hawk and stay out of reach
You laugh out loud telling the world of your scorn for me
Your disdain is my tomb of limestone in a dead world

You are that kind of woman

You reach out across the seconds and hours to find me
But I am alert as a hawk and stay out of reach
I am unable to speak words of honesty I don't believe in
My words are walls I am too afraid to tear it down

I am that kind of man

Maybe we have a standoff
Between the cab driver's son
And the professor's daughter

Sad Cup of Coffee

While politicians were
running around
Reinventing Jesus as an American
In a honky-tonk bar in Brooks
A country singer was singing a song about a sad cup of coffee
Sitting at a table was a Townes Van Zandt
He looked at his coffee
And said to himself
   I've had a cold cup of coffee
   I've had a hot cup of coffee
   I've had good and bad cups of coffee
   But I've never had a sad cup of coffee
He pushed the coffee aside
And from the pocket on the inside
Of his jean jacket
He pulled out a micky of Jack Daniels

At the next table was Roger Gates
A pyro-technician
He looked at his coffee
And thought to himself
   What kind of name is Roger for a pyro-technician

he said do you need a dollar

corner of broadway & memorial boulevard
stood a panhandler on the median
he had a cardboard sign in his hands
anything would help   god bless

as my pickup truck   (yes i drive a pickup)
came to a stop for the red light
the panhandler stepped toward me

i indicated i had no change

he came to my rolled down window
seeing me is just enough he sd

i sd i only had a quarter

he put a hand into his left pocket
he said   do you need a dollar

i gave him my only 25 cents

i wish he had given me that dollar

Copyright Infringement

"Every unhappy family is unhappy in its own way."
I wrote that.
Then I find out that Tolstoy
Used my words, my words, in Anna Karina.

Well, I sicced my lawyer after him.
Did not answer.
Ignored the subpoenas.

What is a poor boy supposed to do?
It was the best of times, it was the worst of times.

Hey!

Monk

Did I live it or did I embellish it?
Was the joint passed to me that I passed onto to Monk,
or did someone hand me the Coca Cola
and told me to pass it along to Monk?
Was I even at the party?

Hanging Sam

Hanging Sam had no joke for his 1000th execution

He thought he might the morning before
But when he got home from Abilene after his 999th execution
He found a Dear John letter tacked to his favorite rocking chair

Jackie Wallas   his lover of 13 years   left him for The Yukon
She heard there was good money to made in Dawson City
If a woman properly applied herself

He cursed Jackie his gangrene Banshee

Hanging Sam conducted his 1000th execution
Like a man who had nothing in his bones

He was no longer numb
Like the other 999
For the 1000th
He was no longer numb

And it pissed him off

While Horseback Riding

Drinking a cup of coffee
While riding a horse
Is not such a good idea
Nor is texting or knitting
Sex okay sure why not
But not performing surgery

Road Kill

He had a thing about road kill.
He even wrote and published a book of recipes
On how to prepare various road kill.

On September 8, 1979,
He became road kill,

But you will never find a recipe in any cookbook
On how to prepare him.

Bus 5612

I have two daughters.
Many years ago
When the oldest was about two years old
I took her by bus to see her grandmother in Selkirk.
A tall East African immigrant boarded the bus
And sat directly behind us.
My daughter stared and stared at him.
Could not take her eyes off of him.
I tried to get her to sit down
But she would immediately stand and stare at him again.
I apologized if she was causing any discomfort.
    As he stood
To get off the bus at the Middlechurch stop,
He said to me,
    "She hasn't seen many of us,
Has she?"

On a Trip to Disney World

On a trip to Disney World
The granddaughter trailed behind her
Grandmother and aunt
When they passed by two young black women
Sitting on a benched outside a landscaped building

The grandmother said loudly
That's the way she spoke
"If they weren't black they'd be pretty"

The aunt looked down and sped up her step
The granddaughter halted and whispered
To the two young black women
Sitting on the bench
"I'm sorry"

The two young black women shrugged their shoulders
And smiled seeming to say
"We are sorry for you"

Pretty Boy Floyd Knew

Water decided to make itself scarce
The unending dry mountain winds was damned to make sure
The rain did not come that summer
The cattle withered on the parched land
The rancher cursed the god he didn't believe in

The situation wasn't any better up north

California was a mess
Georgia wasn't so peachy

The sheep were sold off first
The cattle later
Ranches were foreclosed

But like time banks were eternal
Found away to make a buck or two or a million
Out of the dried blood of the ranchers

Pretty Boy Floyd knew that
And he knew how to make the bankers scream

Family Album

Just because he murdered 6 people
Doesn't make him a bad boy

Said the mother
Before she plugged him

What runs in the family
Stays in the family

The Rains Came Down

The rains came down
But it came too late
He died along ago with his crops and livestock

The rains came down
But it did his son no good
He rode with Pretty Boy Floyd
The G-men shot him down outside of Tulsa

The rains came down
But did his wife no good
On her way back from the funeral
The sheriff was knocking on her door
The bank was foreclosing on the farm

The rains came down
But if did no one any good

The land died in those years

Family Album

Just because he murdered 6 people
Doesn't make him a bad boy

Said the mother
Before she plugged him

What runs in the family
Stays in the family

The Rains Came Down

The rains came down
But it came too late
He died along ago with his crops and livestock

The rains came down
But it did his son no good
He rode with Pretty Boy Floyd
The G-men shot him down outside of Tulsa

The rains came down
But did his wife no good
On her way back from the funeral
The sheriff was knocking on her door
The bank was foreclosing on the farm

The rains came down
But if did no one any good

The land died in those years

Poem for Franklyn

It was my first full day in Santa Monica.
I was walking on the Santa Monica pier when he approached me.
"Spare a cigarette," he asked.
I gave him one. Lit it with my bic lighter. He asked me,
    "Are you from California?"
    "No, I'm from Canada."
    "I am from Chicago.
      It's too cold to sleep on the street in Chicago.
      My name is Franklin"
    "I'm Grant."
He dragged on the cigarette.
    "Met any California women?"
    "No, I sputtered. I only arrived last night."
He politely wished me well and left.

The next day he approached me,
    "Got an extra cigarette?"
I gave him one.
    "Met any California women yet?"
    "No."
    "Me neither."
He wandered off as he dragged on the cigarette.

Every day for the next two weeks
Franklin asked me for a cigarette, and always asked,
    "Met any California women yet?
    "No," was my answer.
He shrugged,
    "Neither have I."

It was my last full day in Santa Monica.
Franklin was making a beeline toward me.
In his hand he was holding two cigarettes.
   "I bummed two cigarettes.
    Let's have our last cigarettes together."
We leaned on the railing.
He silently puffed on the cigarette.
      "Met any California women yet?"
   "No."
Franklin beamed.
   "I did. She's from San Diego.
    We share a locker at the bus depot."

All She Ate

All She Ate Was Skin
The family Christmas was not a happy time
Buried rancour gave birth to whimpering silence
Christ's birth was a death sentence on the ode of joy
It was the same every Christmas
It remained like this every Christmas until
Everyone was filling their plates with turkey
Swedish meatballs
Mashed potatoes
Salad
Store bought buns
Brussels sprouts
Gravy
Until Auntie Myrtle cried out
If you do not want your turkey skin
Save it for Pammy

Hell

The last thing
The frog sees
When the Northern Pike
Is eating it
Is the Northern Pike.
Now that is Hell.

When you catch a Northern Pike
The last thing it sees
Before it dies
Is you.
Now that is Hell.

The last thing I see
Deep sea diving off the coast of Australia
When the white shark
Is eating me
Is the white shark.
Now that is hell.

She Just Did

He worked Old Man Cassels ranch
He knew more about sheep than any man in the panhandle
Other than that, he was not worth more than a plug of tobacca
His wife never knew why she loved him

He was no Douglas Fairbanks
    She knew other men before him
And most were far better
      at the art of lovemaking
    at the art of sex

He never drank much
Never talked loudly
It might be because of the way his eyes smiled
When he looked at her
It might have been the way he held her hand
Sitting on the front porch watching the sun go down
It might have been the way he loved her unconditionally
He never took away her freedom

She didn't know why she loved him

        She just did

It Is Best

It is best
When tossing cow chips
That they are dry.

A Wider World

Behind
A plow horse
The world looks
Much wider.

Hymn for Pat Garrett

Would ya believe it
His lawyer from Boston called it self-defense
'N the judge agreed
Here Ah were
Takin' a leak agin the back wheel on my buckboard
'N the ol' coyote spit
Assassinated me in the back ov my head
In the back ov my head, Ah tell ya
Ah ne'er knew my piss were a deadly weapon

1959

She said
    You don't like anything
    After 1959

He said
    That's not true
    I like The Man From U.N.C.L.E

Times Are Always the Same
    'Cept When Times A'changin'

Time are always the same 'cept when times a'changin'

Grandpappy always told Kid Bonney
But the Kid knew that
He were the time's a'changin' in flesh
'N he were only 20 years old
Time's a'changin' at that age

He would be immortal if he could play the guitar 'n sing
He might've been the Bob Dylan of his age
But he didn't n' couldn't
But he were good with his six-shooter

Took out his first man who were abusin' him
Big man too n' the Kid were no more
than 5'4" n' 115 soakin' wet

The Kid stood up fer his friends
He cherished loyalty but were hurt by friends
who turned agin him
Stood up fer those shat upon
But they shouldn't expect the Kid to be good ever

The Kid were the times a'changin'
'Til Pat Garrett closed mouth Pat Garrett
Who knows what Pat Garrett did on that day
Pat Garrett ain't talkin'
Not 'cause he were dead

Pat Garrett cloaked himself with loyalty

Baked Beans With Crow

A good-hearted woman and a two-timing man
Are the perfect recipe for a country & western hit
But eating baked beans with crow

At the Rawhide Honky-Tonk
Don't brag about how many cows you punched
Or how many dogies you got-a-long
    No one's gonna be listening to you

Folks come here to get drunk fast and cheap
Or look for the empty love

1875

Riding across the invisible line
That divided Alberta from Montana
She sat high in the saddle
She looked out upon the spreading world in front of her

The view was fine.

She knew the world could not remain the way it was.
High in the saddle she was changing the world.
Ever other woman who had and
We're going to ride high in the saddle
Or broke the earth with an oxen pulled plow
Would change the world.

Bunchgrass

Bunchgrass knew more about life
On the relentless and unforgiving plains
With its smiling and unforgiving sun

And   It took no prisoner   winter
He knew that

He thought highly of the bunchgrass's skills
And it's pioneering skills of stamina

But under the heavy hand of nature
He thought highly of his mustang
If he were to survive out here in endless stretches
Of time and space
It would be the mustang his saviour.

John Symons

She had something for John Symons
The man she did not find handsome
Yet somehow in his clumsy manner
He made her feel like the only woman in the world

When unhappy with pointless endless lines of loves
Refused in their stubborn way to make her happy
She thought of John Symons who was always there for her
That kept her faith that happiness was achievable

When John Symons died in his sixty-sixth year
She at sixty-three was the only one at his grave side
She smiled because she recalled how he made her feel
Like she was the only woman in the world his world

For that she was happy

Poem No 4

Outside a horse with no name
Inside was Betsy Deloraine
Who had the name of a thousand cowboys'
Tattooed on her soul

For fifteen dollars
That was the price of her fame
She made each cowboy think
He was her only one

For 10 minutes at least

Poem No 5

Sunday afternoon came too late
He did the Deadman's dance Saturday morning

It was too late now to regret his actions
If he could he would but now he couldn't

The barkeep told him Miss Molly was the sheriff's woman
But after eleven shots of whiskey albeit watered down
No warning of a barkeep could cut through the haze of alcohol

When he said to Miss Molly
I love your ass   it was bigger than big sky country
I like big asses
He was in earshot of Sheriff Templeton

Propositioning the sheriff's woman during her off hours
Was a capital crime in the opinion of the sheriff
No man in her off hours could speak to her like that
If he had paid his two dollars like any other cowboy
During Miss Molly's working hours
He might have gone to church Sunday

But he never owned a watch

Cowboy Art

He looked upon his plate of baked beans an' prairie oysters

Why did he ever decide to become a cowboy
He had a talent for drawing
His Grade 6 teacher told him he were a natural artist
Push yourself   Go to Paris an' become a real artist
    like that Van Gogh fella
But poppa weren't havin' any of that talk
Poppa took his son out to the barn
Tied him to a post an' whipped his son with a rope
No son of mine were goin' to be a soft boy
So he became a cowboys' tead an artist like that Van Gogh fella

His momma cries to this day thinkin' what poppa did to the boy
But if she said anythin' poppa would whip her
That's the kind of man he were

But the cowboy lookin' down on his baked beans
   an' prairie oysters
Promised to treat no wife of his
Like poppa beat momma
Even if he were a cowboy
He were gonna be a different kind of cowboy

A Buffalo Rode
Across His Soul Each Night

A buffalo rode across his soul each night
Why not   He killed it for no reason but fun

Why He killed it for no reason but fun

Other folks from Lawrence, Kansas
Did exactly the same thing
And the government did nothing to stop him

But Now Today

Every echo of the boom of a buffalo gun
Increases the thunder of the dead buffalo
That rode across his soul each night
But did he care then

But Now Today

A buffalo rides across his soul each night
Why He killed it for no reason but fun
Why doesn't the government do something about it
He killed for no reason but for fun
Where is the sin in that He asked
Where is the sin in that

A buffalo rides across his soul each night

Why

He Was Thirsty the Day He Died

He was thirsty on the day he died
Although he camped by a cool stream
The water was beyond his reach
And the vigilantes had no plans
To bring him any closer to the water
They let him kick and swing
From the branch of the tree
Gasping for air he could not swallow

It did not matter if he was guilty or innocent
That was not the concern of the vigilantes

Lynching was their game

Butch Cassidy

Butch Cassidy was a good guy
Butch Cassidy was a bad guy
Whatever he was he became an anachronism
A man out of time
A man the present left him behind
Technology was his antichrist
So Bolivia
Bolivia he went
The good guy
The bad guy
Bolivia was in his chronology

He Had Dreams

His father would have walked out on him
But he beat his father to the punch
He had his dreams   big dreams
When he hit the road in the language of Kerouac
Kenneth Patchen was the star he followed
The apex he would exceed
But that was 30 years ago
He works at Hill Home Hardware in Medicine Hat
And no one remembers his name

He Danced at the Drop of a Note

He danced at the drop of a note
A cool note
A blue note

& the note floated out into the audience
& landed in my heart & soul

He changed me forever
At the DNA level
When I left the concert i was not
The same person that went in
& i have danced the urban folk song

Since

In a Small Hotel Room

In a small town hotel
Lumberjacks and hydro workers
Find love by the hour
In the shadow of mercantile love
Two honest bodies found themselves
And sang each other's song

The Beatnik Cowboy

the beatnik cowboy hd a cashmere heartache
for his Dale Evans who set up house in exurbia
with a wallet full of tax exemptions

but
not all was sweet love in the loft
she said she hd it up to here with art
(she indicated her chin that already showed signs of doubling)
art was the root ov her big sky agony

she sd as she slammed out ov their loft
he cld shove his bongos up his ass

shove my bongos up my ass
He sd
i have a James Dean ass
impossible
a shiver rocked his flesh

Hobo

I got nuthin' & nuthin's got me
So why all the long faces
I follow the highways
& the railways
& the sun & moon & the days & years
All the same if you don't keep track

Today I'm Tom
Tomorrow I will be Bill
Just last week I was Gene
Next Tuesday I think I will be Sam
When I'm paid I'm paid in cash
John Dough that's me

There is a freedom not ownin' anythin'
Not against or for anythin'
You're not even against Death
It is part of my nuthin'

I got it made

I ain't no bum

I'm a
Hobo

Hobo
Pretty good
Hey

The Tall Prairie Grass
Was in His Language

Tall prairie grass was in his language
The unending sky was in his blood
How he howled

He walked a path now his
(Walked by ancestors not his)
By virtue of blood dried atonement yet gained
How he howled

For the ghosts of those ancestors
For the ghosts of the living
For himself
How he howled

In the air   In his soul
He wanted to dance the dance of atonement
He could not dance   But he could not dance
How he howled

he can walk

in the middle of the night
between truck stops
& 3:00 am waitresses
unimaginable monsters await at underpasses
aliens from outer space hover beyond
to levitate me into their flying saucer
& just ahead jesus is thumbing a ride
he could keep me company
maybe share the driving.
we could talk about our favorite wines
wedding parties & parents

o christ
he is wearing a baseball cap

ah fuck it
he can walk

Fathers

he a taxi drive applied all his talents to the job
he knew every brothel bootlegger and bookie joint in town
he knew every street every avenue back alley
like his name and the back of his hand

but he could never remember his son's birthday
nor had he met any of his son's friend

the son put distance between himself and his father

the day his grade 8 teacher told him
don't aspire beyond what your parents
that is the place where God meant you to be

that was the day the son lost faith
in all fathers real or imagined

When my father mounted my mother

when my father mounted my mother
it was domestic rape
but she was gonna give him a son
come hell / high water
goddamn you you bitch

i was to be the replacement son
you know for the one that died

i never became the replacement son
i was a disappointment

i dont think my dead brother
wld have matched up to my fathers' idea of a son
both the living & dead wld disappoint the old man
he went out & found another woman to plant his seed in
& she gave him a son
but my mother made damn sure
my father wld never see his son
come hell or high water
goddamn you you bastard
the husband & the wife
hated each other more than god
& the devil hated each other
& my dead brother
& the brother i never met

& i
paid the price of admission

Picture Of Jesus

He asked the librarian
Do you have any pictures of Jesus
The librarian led him to the religious section 200s
And showed him pictures of Jesus

No no
He said
You don't understand
I want pictures of Jesus

The librarian steered him to the art section 700s
And showed him pictures painted by famous artists

No no
He said in exasperation
You don't understand
I want pictures of Jesus

The librarian said
I showed you pictures of Jesus
How Jesus has been depicted through the centuries

That's the problem
He said
I don't want a depiction of Jesus

I want a picture of Jesus
A photograph

Going Out for Ice Cream

His father didn't think much of his son
But that's okay because the son never thought of the father

But that did not stop them
For going out for ice cream
On different days
And in different cities

Neither was fond of vanilla

Mingus

the evening star
stared
    &
stared
at him
rage of hope mingus

the evening star
sang
    &
sang
the blues to him
rage of hope mingus

Poem No 8

I am a nowhere I am everywhere
I am with you from your first breath to your last
I am with for your needs I have no hand to lend

I am not your friend

I don't give a damn about you I own your soul
You will succumb to me I never look at you
I have a plan for you I lead you astray

I am not your engine

I roll the dice you never know where I tossed them
I open doors for you I stand in your way
I provide the red carpet I pull the rug out from under you

I am not your friend
I am not your engine
I get in the way of your living

I am Life I get in the way

I Life get in the way of living

I Drink Hard Enough
When I Am Sober

I drink hard enough when I am sober
And I burn all my bridges
And I know there's a woman out there
Who loves me

&

I will never love her

This is known facts to me
But when I come to climb on the train
To take me away from here it will be late
And it's speed and location are unknown

It is the roll of the dice in the dark
That gives my uncertainty meaning

Nothing to Say to the World

His eyes have nothing to say to the world
And they are very happy that way thank you very much
His eyes have turned a dead man's eyes
Looking at us and away from us

If they wanted speak what would they say
Fuck you and go to hell
Or I will die at too early of an age
Or just turn to stone silence glass
Or will they walk to the death chamber

Without a word of remorse or fear of God
Inside the eyes only the eyes know what they are thinking
And even that is holding its tongue

Grant Guy is a Winnipeg, Canada, poet, writer, and playwright. Former artistic director of *Adhere + Deny*. His poems, short stories, essays and art criticism have been published in Canada, United States, Wales, India, Scotland, Africa, and England.

He has three books published: *Open Fragments (Lives of Dogs)*, *On the Bright Side of Down* and *Bus Stop Bus Stop "Red Dashboard"*. His plays include *A.J. Loves B.B.*, *Song for Simone* and an adaptation of *Paradise Lost and the Grand Inquisitor*. He was the 2004 recipient of the *MAC's Award of Distinction* and the 2017 recipient of the *WAC's Making A Difference Award*.

www.thereddahliapress.com

Home of the Red Dahlia Chapbook Prize